OECD Public Governance Reviews

Review of the Kazakhstan Commission on Access to Information

)) OECD

BETTER POLICIES FOR BETTER LIVES

This work is published under the responsibility of the Secretary-General of the OECD. The opinions expressed and arguments employed herein do not necessarily reflect the official views of OECD member countries.

This document, as well as any data and map included herein, are without prejudice to the status of or sovereignty over any territory, to the delimitation of international frontiers and boundaries and to the name of any territory, city or area.

Please cite this publication as:
OECD (2020), *Review of the Kazakhstan Commission on Access to Information*, OECD Public Governance Reviews, OECD Publishing, Paris, *https://doi.org/10.1787/3a8d6a0e-en*.

ISBN 978-92-64-58192-0 (print)
ISBN 978-92-64-36461-5 (pdf)

OECD Public Governance Reviews
ISSN 2219-0406 (print)
ISSN 2219-0414 (online)

Foreword

Open government promotes the principles of transparency, integrity, accountability and stakeholder participation in support of democracy and inclusive growth. Countries around the world increasingly acknowledge that open government can improve government efficiency and effectiveness, while bringing the administration and its officials closer to citizens.

Kazakhstan has been working to make its government more open, and to better engage citizens and civil society in the policy-making process. To this end, it established a Commission on Access to Information.

In 2017, the OECD conducted an Open Government Review of Kazakhstan as part of its Kazakhstan Country Programme. The review recommended mainstreaming the principles of transparency, accountability, integrity, and stakeholder participation in the country's ongoing public sector reform process. In order to support the implementation of those recommendations, the OECD was asked to evaluate Kazakhstan's new Commission on Access to Information against OECD principles and best practices.

Drawing on OECD's extensive experience, this report assesses the law on access to information of the Republic of Kazakhstan in line with OECD standards and benchmarks the functions of the Kazakhstan Commission on Access to Information against those of similar access to information oversight bodies in relevant OECD countries. The analysis included a comparison of the legal nature, institutional structure and functioning of these institutions, with a focus on the presence and effectiveness of appeal mechanisms.

The findings presented in this report show that, unlike access to information oversight bodies in OECD member countries, Kazakhstan's Commission lacks institutional and financial autonomy and is not legally empowered to effectively oversee the implementation of the law, especially with respect to decisions denying citizens' access to information requests.

To address these differences and bring the Kazakhstan Commission closer to those of OECD countries, the Review proposes broadening the Commission's mandate and reconsidering its institutional position under the Ministry of Information and Communications. It also suggests strengthening the Commission by including more representatives from civil society and academia, establishing a code of conduct and requiring higher academic qualifications of its members.

Acknowledgements

This report was prepared by the OECD Public Governance Directorate (GOV) under the leadership of Marcos Bonturi, Director. It was written by Richard Martinez in collaboration with Hille Hinsberg, Policy Analyst of the OECD Open Government Unit, as part of the Kazakhstan Country programme. It was drafted under the supervision of Alessandro Bellantoni, Head of the Open Government Unit and Martin Forst, Head of the Governance Reviews and Partnerships Division of GOV. Amelia Godber provided editorial support.

The OECD wishes to acknowledge the significant contribution made by their interlocutors in the Republic of Kazakhstan. In particular, the Deputy Head of Policy Department Mr. Bekzat Rakhimov and Chief Policy Expert on Access to Information, Ms. Elmira Nurkisheva, of the Ministry for Information and Communications.

Table of contents

Tables

Boxes

Abbreviations and acronyms

ATIL	Law of the Republic of Kazakhstan of the 16th of November 2015 "On Access to Information".
CADA	Commission for Access to Administrative Documents
CATI	Commission on Access to Information of the Republic of Kazakhstan
CNIL	Commission nationale de l'informatique et des libertés – French Data Protection body
FOI	Freedom of Information laws
OECD	Organisation for Economic Co-operation and Development
NGO	Non-governmental organisation
OSCE	Organisation for Security and Cooperation in Europe
SDGs	Sustainable Development Goals

Executive Summary

Kazakhstan is taking continuous steps towards greater openness, striving to ensure the transparency of government-held data and proactively publishing information and official documents, including through digital channels. However, like many other countries around the world, Kazakhstan faces complex challenges on the path towards open government, which the OECD defines as a "culture of governance based on innovative and sustainable public policies and practices inspired by the principles of transparency, accountability, and participation that fosters democracy and inclusive growth."

Enabling policy and legal framework for transparency

The government of the Republic of Kazakhstan has expressed a strong commitment to enhancing the transparency, accountability and participation in the policy-making process to reinforce public trust and improve the quality of public services. As part of the Kazakhstan 2050 Strategy, the government is undertaking five institutional reforms to help the country strengthen the capacity of the state and fulfil its objective to become one of the 30 most developed countries in the world by 2050. One of these five institutional reforms focuses on "Transparency and Accountability of the State" and exemplifies the administration's commitment to open government reforms.

Kazakhstan has passed an access to information law, which is commonly recognised as a fundamental pillar of a transparent and accountable public administration. However, additional steps are required to ensure its proper implementation and oversight. For example, OECD practice suggests that, to promote the effective implementation of the law, the Access to Information Commission should have legal responsibility and operative, budgetary and decision-making autonomy, and that it should report to the legislature.

The role of oversight mechanisms

There is no specific obligation under international law to create an oversight body such as an Information Commission, an Information Commissioner or an Ombudsman. However, these functions are exercised, with varying degrees of specialisation, by different institutions in all OECD countries. Experience generally shows that oversight institutions play a fundamental role in promoting a culture of transparency and access to information, support the implementation of related policies and legal provisions, and increase compliance. The Access to Information Commission in Kazakhstan should have a similar oversight role.

Improving the functions of the Commission

The law establishes that Kazakhstan's Information Commission is an administrative body with an advisory role that is not empowered to rule on individual decisions regarding the refusal of access to information. This is in contrast with all access to information commissions in OECD countries. Moreover, its *modus operandi* and internal functioning could be better aligned to OECD principles and best practices by increasing the transparency of its operations, creating a repository of its decisions and making these accessible to the public, drafting annual reports to be presented to the Parliament, and collaborating more with all other entities tasked with ensuring access to information.

Recommendations requiring changes in legislation

Considering the important differences between the OECD's oversight bodies for access to information and the Information Commission in Kazakhstan, some measures are recommended in the report that would require legislative changes.

These changes would include creating a more inclusive selection of the members of the Commission by, for example, engaging more representatives from civil society and academia. Moreover, it is recommended to reinforce the professional obligations of its members by drafting a code of conduct and increasing the academic qualifications required of members.

In addition, it is recommended to consider modifying the Commission's mandate by entrusting it with new functions, including the possibility of deciding on appeals in the event of a refusal of access to information by institutions of the executive branch.

Finally, reconsidering the Commission's institutional positioning should be a priority. Currently, it is chaired by the Deputy Prime Minister and it operates under the Ministry of Information and Communications, which do not guarantee its independence.

Introduction

Article 18 of the Constitution of the Republic of Kazakhstan establishes: [...] "3. State bodies, public associations, officials, and the mass media must provide every citizen with the possibility to obtain access to documents, decisions and other sources of information concerning his rights and interests." Article 20 of the Constitution states: "2. Everyone shall have the right to freely receive and disseminate information by any means not prohibited by law. The list of items constituting state secrets of the Republic of Kazakhstan shall be determined by law."

In May 2015, President of the Republic of Kazakhstan Nursultan Nazarbayev announced a "Plan of the Nation" to radically change the country with 100 concrete steps implementing 5 institutional reforms (creation of a modern and professional civil service; ensuring the rule of law; industrialisation and economic growth; a unified nation for the future; transparency and accountability of the state). The 94th step provides the introduction of "the open government" and commits to drafting a law on access to information that will allow access to any information of state agencies, except for highly confidential state documents and other information protected by law.

In this context, on 16 November 2015, Kazakhstan passed an Access to Information Law (ATIL). Although the drafting process was inclusive and benefited from the participation of local NGOs and international organisations, the law passed in 2015 received some criticism. The same year, the Government of Kazakhstan established a Commission on Access to Information (CATI) having to ensure the right to access information as per the ATIL (by Resolution No. 1175 of 31 December 2015).

Regulations guiding the mandate and operations of the CATI are the Law of the Republic of Kazakhstan "On Access to Information", the Resolution of the Government of the Republic of Kazakhstan "On Approval of the Regulations on the Procedure for the Activity of the Commission", the Resolution of the Government "On Approval of the Instruction on the Procedure for Establishment, Operation and Liquidation of Consultative and Advisory Bodies under the Government of the Republic of Kazakhstan".

The commission began its work in 2016, and has held its meetings regularly, at least once a year (four meetings have been held between 2016 and 2018).

The Commission is an advisory body under the Ministry of Information and Communications. The Ministry is the working body of the Commission. The composition of the Commission was approved by the order of the Minister of Information and Communications. The current Chair of the Commission is the Deputy Prime Minister of the Republic of Kazakhstan.

The Commission's decisions are of a recommendatory nature. Decisions taken at the meeting of the Commission are registered in the official minutes and sent for execution to state bodies and organisations. The Chairman exercises overall control over the implementation of the decisions of the Commission. In practice, most of the decisions taken by the Commission have concerned the Ministry of Information and Communications itself.

Chapter 1. Oversight bodies for access to information

Types of oversight bodies for access to information

The notion of access to information lies between two, somewhat opposite legal concepts:

- The protection of personal data;
- The access to information.

On the one side, the term refers to the right generally or specifically held by individuals or legal entities to obtain all communicable information under the law or certain items of information that concern them in particular. On the other side, the notion pertains to the right of persons not to have information concerning them be disclosed, modified, or aggregated, especially through any automated processing to which such data may be subject.

OECD countries have passed legislation on the right to access information and established institutions guaranteeing the right to access information. These entities play a fundamental role in the promotion, application, and growth of this right, as well as in the protection of personal data and the communication of documents and information (OECD, 2019).

From an institutional point of view, the oversight functions to guarantee the right to access information and protect personal data may be carried out by a single institution or separately by at least two institutions. Sometimes the functions are performed by an institution that also performs other functions. In organisational terms, there are four kinds of institutions in OECD countries:

- An Ombudsman or Mediator (for example, in Sweden, Norway, and New Zealand);
- An Information Commissioner (for example, in the United Kingdom, Slovenia, Hungary, Scotland, and Germany);
- A commission or institution (for example, in France, Italy, Portugal, Mexico, and Chile);
- Another body responsible for monitoring this right, such as the Right to Information Assessment Review Council and the Ombudsman in Turkey, both of which ensure the observance of all relevant laws.

The mission and functions of an oversight body for access to information

The right of access to information has constitutional and conventional foundations in OECD countries. However, there is no provision in international law requiring the creation of an oversight body for access to information.

All OECD countries have a body to review the right of access to information. The constitution of some OECD countries provides for the creation of an oversight body for access to information, but most of these institutions have been created by law or executive order.

Among OECD countries, some oversight bodies for access to information are competent only for legislation regarding the disclosure of information, and other bodies are competent for legislation regarding the protection of personal data during their collection, processing and storage. Some oversight bodies combine these two functions, while other bodies are also responsible for additional functions.

Some access to information oversight bodies take the form of single-person entities, such as ombudsmen or information commissioners, while others are collegial institutions, such as access to information commissions.

To facilitate the application of laws on the right to access information, national legislation authorises oversight bodies to provide their opinions, recommendations, and counsel to the authorities and all individuals involved in the law's application. Generally, these institutions have the power to produce studies and reports, and to formulate general observations and proposals for action (see Box 1.1)

Institutions often have the right to conduct investigations at their own initiative to formulate their observations.

Box 1.1. Information policy of the Australian Information Commissioner

The Office of the Australian Information Commissioner (OAIC) has responsibility for advising the Australian Government on Information Policy.

The OAIC supports the development of effective information policy by:

- Providing advice about best practice information policy to government

- Developing resources to assist government agencies implement best practice information policy

- Influencing policy through submissions

- Consulting with government about the challenges they face in information policy

- Consulting with the private sector, researchers, advocates and the community about how the value and use of public sector information can be maximised

- Conducting research into information policy international best practice.

Source: Australian Information Commissioner https://www.oaic.gov.au/information-policy/

Requests for access to information

The processing of requests to access information is of primary importance to the work of an oversight body. It entails the examination and consideration of complex legal issues. This function is granted by the relevant legislation on access to information. The institution is authorised to give its opinion on all aspects of this legislation in relation to the individual or collective situations it may review. It specifically provides its opinion on the grounds for the refusal to communicate any information, and often on the possibility of its reuse, especially in Europe.

The free nature of access to information is becoming the rule, or at the very least, the relative cost does not exceed an acceptable threshold. Penalties for the undue communication of information vary depending on individual laws and practices. Similarly, exceptions to the right to access information remain significant in some countries, and the institutions often provide their opinion on these exceptions. An official decision is generally based on three principles: the protection or privacy and national security, the concept of on-going matters, and the correctness of the application.

The specific purpose of piece of information's accessibility or inaccessibility is to protect the legitimate interests of certain individuals or, more generally, those of society as a whole. For example, whistle-blowers must benefit from specific, adequate protections.

The modes of recourse against refusals of access to information and the legal grounds that grant people the right to consult an oversight body vary from one OECD member country to another. In case of an explicit or tacit refusal, some legal systems authorise the victim of the refusal to file an appeal before a court, or to appeal to an oversight body. Other legal systems, such as France's, require that the person apply to the oversight body before bringing any legal proceedings.

When an oversight body receives a request to access information, it issues an administrative, public, or judicial decision. It may in some cases allow for a partial communication of the information.

The functioning of an oversight body

Single-person bodies are in most cases structured around a representative, information commissioner, or ombudsman. This person manages an office and may receive support from a council. Collegial institutions are composed of several members who hold the same hierarchical level, make collective decisions, and are managed by a chairperson.

Usually, oversight bodies are supported by administrative departments whose personnel and organisation generally reflect the diversity of their missions. These bodies that are responsible solely for access to information are smaller in size and have a relatively simple organisation. When the oversight body has a greater number of functions, the amount of staff increases and the organisational chart becomes more complex.

Depending on the traditions and legislation, the institutions enact procedures with varying degrees of formality to introduce, review, and rule on access to information, both in general and specifically concerning one or more individuals.

Oversight bodies enjoy considerable autonomy in their operations. Their budgets differ widely in function of their missions, size, and the specific situation of each state or inter-state group.

Oversight of the work of institutions guaranteeing access to information

Even though the institutions are independent, they are subject to oversight, as all public bodies should be. They are exempt from the hierarchical control of the head of their department and the actions of the supervisory body within the executive branch, but, depending on the country's legislation, they may be subject to different forms of external oversight of an administrative or judicial nature.

Whether or not an oversight body reports to the Parliament, it remains under its oversight, either by virtue of the parliamentary oversight of the executive branch or directly, for example, as part of the compilation and review of the annual budget. Some bodies submit their reports directly to the Parliament, which may debate them.

Different types of judicial recourse against the actions of an oversight body are also possible, depending on the legal system of each OECD member country.

Legal grounds for creating an oversight body for access to information

There is no specific obligation under international law to create an oversight body such as an Information Commission, an Information Commissioner or an Ombudsman. At the General Assembly in September 2015, the member states of the United Nations adopted Agenda 2030, formulated to guide global and national development policies for the next 15 years. Agenda 2030 includes 17 Sustainable Development Goals (SDGs), each with multiple specific targets. Among these targets is SDG 16.10, which obliges signatory countries to "ensure public access to information and protect fundamental freedoms, in accordance with national legislation and international agreements".

The Organisation for Security and Cooperation in Europe (OSCE), the Council of Europe and the OECD have also adopted several documents pertaining to oversight bodies for access to information.

In its May 2007 review of the right of access to information, the Organisation for Security and Cooperation in Europe, of which Kazakhstan is a member, included the existence of a dedicated oversight body in its analysis of the core elements of the right, and it recommended all member states to create such a body. The review document explained that "There should be an adequate mechanism for appealing each refusal to disclose. This should include having an independent oversight body such as an Ombudsman or Commission which can investigate and order releases. The body should also promote and educate on freedom of information." (OSCE, 2007)

The Council of Europe in its 2002 Recommendation on Access to Official Documents states in its Principle IX that "An applicant whose request for an official document has been refused, whether in part or in full, or dismissed, or has not been dealt with within the time limit […] should have access to a review procedure before a court of law or another independent and impartial body established by law."

Recommendation of the Council of the OECD on Open Government declares that adherents should "Ensure the existence and implementation of the necessary open government legal and regulatory framework, including through the provision of supporting documents such as guidelines and manuals, while establishing adequate oversight mechanisms to ensure compliance" (OECD, 2017b).

In summary:

- Kazakhstan has no legal international obligation to create an oversight body for access to information;

- There is no mandatory principle or specific recommendation by the OECD to compel Kazakhstan to establish an oversight body for access to information.

The creation of an oversight body for access to information in the legislation of Kazakhstan

Creation of the commission on access to information

Kazakhstan's constitution does not provide for the obligation to create a body to monitor the right of access to information. It was the Law of the Republic of Kazakhstan of 16 November 2015 "On Access to Information" that established such a body. The Law in its Article 19 provides general provisions allowing the creation of the CATI: "in order to account for and defend public interests in the field of access to information, and also in order to satisfy the demands of information users, a consultative-advisory body or commission on issues of access to information is formed within the structure of a designated body, determined by the Government of the Republic of Kazakhstan".

Other institutions responsible for ensuring the right of access to information and data protection

The right of access to information covers a range of aspects, and different institutions can be mandated to ensure protection of this right.

Law on access to information

Article 18 of the Law provides: "Decisions and actions (inactions) of information holders, including a governmental body, a local self-government, an organisation, an official, a public servant, violating the rights of information users may be appealed against in a superior body, to a superior official, and/or in court."

Law on personal data protection

Kazakhstan passed the law on Personal Data Protection, dated May 21, 2013 No. 94-V. The liability for violation of that law is both administrative and criminal. When the infringements occur in Kazakhstan, the prosecutor's office is responsible for supervising the implementation of that law and initiating administrative proceedings for its violation.

For violations of personal data protection that happen abroad, any person may address his/her claims to the Ministry of Internal Affairs of Kazakhstan or its territorial departments. Such measures include banning access to Kazakhstan for foreign websites which contain illegally obtained personal data (Colibri Kazakhstan LLP, 2016).

In summary:

- The law on Personal Data Protection does not create a special body to carry out oversight for its execution, investigate possible violations of the law and impose sanctions. These tasks are entrusted to the judiciary and the government.

- The executive power of the Republic of Kazakhstan has wide competencies for the nature, objectives, competencies, powers and organisation of the CATI.

References

Colibri Kazakhstan LLP. Kazakhstan: Personal data protection. Article published on August 4, 2016. Website accessed on September 12, 2018 http://www.mondaq.com/x/516624/Data+Protection+Privacy/Security+As+A+Measure+Of+Comfort+For+Cre ditors,

OECD (2019), Institutions guaranteeing access to information in OECD member countries and in the MENA Region countries, OECD Public Governance Reviews, OECD Publishing, Paris, forthcoming.

OSCE (2007), Access to information by the media in the OSCE region: trends and recommendations.

Chapter 2. The legal nature and composition of CATI

Nature of the CATI

In accordance with Article 19 of the ATIL, the Government of the Republic of Kazakhstan adopted Resolution No. 1175 of 31 December 2015 concerning the regulation of the CATI's rules of procedure. Article 1, paragraph 1 of that resolution establishes that the CATI must respect and protect the public interests in the domain of access to information and meet the needs of information users. Article 1, paragraph 2, provides that "The Commission is a consultative and advisory body under the Ministry of Information and Communications of the Republic of Kazakhstan".

The other main regulation applied to the Commission is the Resolution of the Government of the Republic of Kazakhstan on the Approval of the Instruction on the Procedure for Establishment, Operation and Liquidation of Consultative and Advisory Bodies under the Government of the Republic of Kazakhstan (as a rule, this is used by state bodies in the case of the creation of an advisory body at the state level, as an analogy of the law, since the decree is applicable to consultative meetings of the Government bodies).

The CATI as a consultative and advisory body

Article 1, paragraph 2, of Resolution No. 1175 provides that the CATI is an advisory body. Furthermore, point 14 of that resolution states that "The decisions of the Commission shall have the character of recommendations".

As a result of these provisions, the Commission's decisions have the following features:

- The Commission is only empowered to give advice and recommendations;
- Its acts are drawn up in the form of a protocol taken during its meeting;
- The decisions are not legally binding for their private or public recipients;
- The decisions are not subject to judicial supervision.

The implementation of access to information oversight bodies' acts

Most often, access to information oversight bodies in OECD countries make a recommendation or issue an opinion that is not binding on the reporting entity. For example, the decisions of the Japan Disclosure and Privacy Review Board are not binding. Similarly, in Denmark and Norway, the Ombudsman's reports are not mandatory. For its part, the French Commission for Access to Administrative Documents (CADA) issues a favourable or unfavourable opinion on the communication of the document. Even when CADA's opinion favours an access, the administration can uphold its initial refusal. As a result, in 2011, 7.3% of CADA's opinions were not followed by the organisations to which they were addressed.

In Quebec the Commission for Access to Information reviews the decisions of public bodies following requests from persons who have been refused either access to an administrative document or access to, or correction of, their personal file. After the hearing, a mandatory judgment is provided.

Some administrative bodies in charge of access have real decision-making power. For example, the Italian Commission for Access to Information has such power and may order an administration to disclose a document. In matters of information relevant to the environment, the Brussels Commission for Access to Information has decision-making power.

Sometimes access to information oversight bodies in OECD countries enjoy special powers to enforce the implementation of their decisions. For instance, CADA in France is entitled to impose fines, though only in cases of the fraudulent re-use of public information. These penalties may amount to 300,000 euros. In Sweden, refusal by a public office or an individual citizen to cooperate with the Ombudsman in certain circumstances constitutes an offence under the jurisdiction of a criminal court.

Even without binding force, the recommendations or opinions of OECD access to information oversight bodies are generally respected by the administration or any other addressee of the act. Indeed, these institutions have a strong moral authority and they are able to publicise their actions or the behaviour of the administration or any other addressee.

Recommendations to support implementation of the CATI decisions

Since May 2018, the CATI has been chaired by the Deputy Prime Minister of the Republic of Kazakhstan. This amendment improves the CATI's status, as on the one hand, the Deputy Prime Minister is a leading political authority, and, on the other hand, his or her decisions are binding on the administration in the areas over which he/she has competence.

However, the appointment of the Deputy Prime Minister as head of CATI reinforces the politicisation of the institution and the sense that it provides a possibility for the administration to assess its own actions.

It is therefore recommended that:

- Decisions by the CATI be well founded, fully justified by law and well-argued, made public and announced to the public;
- CATI decision-making procedures be transparent and consistent;
- Its decisions establish a coherent case law that inspires the administration's action.

Legislation on membership in the access to information oversight bodies

Terms of appointment

Resolutions of the Kazakhstan government determine that the CATI is chaired by the Deputy Prime Minister and that its vice-president is the Minister of Information and Communications. The other rules for the appointment of the CATI's members are determined by Resolution of the Government of the Republic of Kazakhstan of 31 December 2015 No. 1175 concerning the approval of the Regulation on the Rules of Procedure of the Commission for Access to Information. Its Article 6 provides: "The commission membership shall be approved by a decree of the Minister of Information and Communications of the Republic of Kazakhstan. […]"

Furthermore Article 10 provides: "The Commission shall include the deputies of the Senate and Mazhilis of the Parliament of the Republic of Kazakhstan, representatives of government authorities and other organisations.

The quantitative and personal composition of the Commission shall be determined at the suggestion of the Commission chairperson upon agreement with the relevant government authorities and other organisations."

The regulations show three groups of CATI members:

- The Deputy Prime Minister and the Minister of Information and Communications, whose appointments to the CATI are individually foreseen;

- Members of the Senate and Mazhilis, whose number is not determined and who should be appointed by their institutions according to the rules they establish, in accordance with the principles of the separation of executive and legislative powers; nevertheless, the legislation could have provided for some appointment rules, for example, to guarantee the representation of the majority and the opposition;

- Other CATI members, the definition of whose quality and qualifications are left to the discretion of the appointing authority.

For the latter group, Articles 6 and 10 of Resolution of 31 December 2015 No. 1175 gives full power of appointment to the Minister of Information and Communications.

The Minister of Information and Communications has the power of appointment, while the CATI is chaired by the Deputy Prime Minister, who is the hierarchical authority for that minister.

Appointment procedures

As noted above, there are several types of access to information oversight bodies in OECD countries. The analysis shows that their appointment procedures vary greatly. However, all these legislations attach the greatest importance to the conditions of appointment, which constitute one of the most important means of ensuring the independence and competence of the authority, and more generally of promoting open governance. For the Commissions, the most common practice in OECD countries is to determine precisely the number of members of the Commission and their conditions of appointment, to limit the discretionary power of the executive branch, and to provide good representation of the citizens.

Furthermore, the access to information oversight bodies' rules of appointment or election of members differ from one institution to another and are largely related to the federal or unitary organisation of the countries, the parliamentary or presidential nature of the regimes, and their institutional traditions. For instance, the four directors of the Chilean Transparency Council are appointed by the President of the Republic, after approval by two thirds of the members of the Senate. In Germany, the Federal Data Protection and Information Commissioner is appointed by the Federal Government. The Scottish Public Services Ombudsman is appointed by the Scottish Parliament. The Council of Ministers (Governor in Council) appoints the Canadian Information Commissioner after consultation with the leader of each of the recognised parties in the Senate and House of Commons and the approval by a simple majority resolution of both assemblies.

The Italian Commission for access to administrative documents is chaired by the Under-Secretary of State in the Presidency of the Council of Ministers. It is also composed of 2 senators and 2 deputies, appointed by the presidents of their respective chambers; 4 judges and lawyers appointed by their respective autonomous bodies; 1 professor teaching Public Affairs and Law, appointed by the Ministry of Education, Universities and Research; and the head of the Presidency of the Council of Ministers, which supports the Commission's operations.

The 11 members of the CADA in France are appointed by a decree of the Prime Minister who merely ratifies appointments made by other authorities or ex officio appointments. For example, the President of the data protection authority (Commission Nationale de l'Informatique et des Libertés, or CNIL) is an ex officio member of the French CADA, and the President of the National Assembly and the President of the Senate respectively appoint a deputy and a senator.

Sometimes the appointment process starts with public calls for applications, like the Scottish Public Services Ombudsman, who is nominated by the Scottish Parliament and appointed by the Queen. In many OECD countries, it is stated that the selection process should appear transparent, open and participatory, leading to the appointment of a person outside political control, supported by civil society and able to gain public trust. Often the selection process involves public hearings, with the establishment of a short list of proposed candidates.

Admittedly, commission composition may be poorly regulated by national legislation, such as the Japanese Disclosure and Privacy Review Commission, composed of 15 experts, chosen and appointed by the Prime Minister from among "persons of superior judgment", which cannot be considered a clear set of criteria.

In summary,

- It is recommended to determine the appointment procedure to the Commission in Kazakhstan's legislation more clearly.

Composition of the Commission

CATI membership

The CATI composition was approved by the order of the Minister of Information and Communications No. 180 of September 29, 2016 (orders no. 234 of February 23, 2018, no. 214 of May 23, 2018, and no. 300 of June 29, 2018 amended the CATI composition) (Table 2.1).

Table 2.1. List of CATI members, with their positions and institutions of origin

Member	Origin
Deputy Prime Minister of the Republic of Kazakhstan, Chairman (as agreed)	
Minister of Information and Communications of the Republic of Kazakhstan, Deputy Chairman	
Vice-Minister of Information and Communications of the Republic of Kazakhstan	
Vice Minister of National Economy of the Republic of Kazakhstan	Members of the Government
Vice Minister of Justice of the Republic of Kazakhstan	
Vice-Minister of the Ministry of Finance of the Republic of Kazakhstan	
Director of the Department of State Policy in the Field of Mass Media of the Ministry of Information and Communications of the Republic of Kazakhstan, Secretary	
Head of the Agency of the Republic of Kazakhstan for Civil Service and Anti-Corruption Affairs	
Chairman of the Information Security Committee of the Ministry of Defence and Aerospace Industry of the Republic of Kazakhstan	Officials of public administration
Deputy Chairman of the Committee on Legal Statistics and Special Records of the Prosecutor General's Office of the Republic of Kazakhstan	
Deputy of the Senate of the Parliament of the Republic of Kazakhstan	
3 Deputies of the Majilis of the Parliament of the Republic of Kazakhstan (by vote)	Members of parliament
Secretary of the party "Nur Otan" (by vote)	Political party
Member of the Board, Deputy Chairman of the Board of the National Chamber of Entrepreneurs of the Republic of Kazakhstan "Atameken" (by vote)	Non-profit non-governmental organisation, union of business entities
Director of the Public Foundation "Center for Economic Analysis" RAKURS (by vote)	Non-governmental organisation
President of the Kazakhstan Association for Internet Development and Resources (by vote)	Private sector association

President of the Public Association "Club of Editors-in-Chief" (by vote)	Non-governmental organisation
Chairman of the Council of the National Movement "Kazakhstan-2050", a member of the National Commission for the Implementation of the Program for Modernisation of Public Consciousness under the President of the Republic of Kazakhstan (by vote)	Civil society
Director of the Institute for Humanitarian Studies and Projects (by vote)	Private research organisation
Deputy Chairman of the Board of the Joint-Stock Company "National Information Technologies" (by vote)	Quasi-governmental organisation
Head of the Program for the Improvement of the Legal Environment in Central Asia of the International Center for Not-for-Profit Law (ICNL)" (by vote)	International research organisation
Lawyer of Internews Kazakhstan (by vote)	International non-profit organisation for the support of independent media

It seems possible to group CATI members into the following categories:

- 6 high-level politicians;
- 4 public officials;
- 5 members of the Parliament and of political parties;
- 2 private organisations;
- 7 non-government and quasi-government organisations, including research organisations;

The CATI decided on the inclusion of representatives of the state bodies and on the scope of their activities; for example, for the Prosecutor General's Office, the issues of legality, for the Ministry of Defence and Aerospace Industry, information security issues, for the Ministry of Finance, the issues of openness in spending budget funds, and for the Ministry of Justice, the regulatory framework.

Composition of oversight bodies for access to information in OECD member countries

The composition of oversight bodies for access to information is quite varied from one country to another, since it may include civil servants, politicians, qualified figures, academics, judges, representatives of civil society, and legal or data protection professionals. For example, France's CADA includes 3 judges (1 from the Council of State, 1 from the Court of Cassation, and 1 from the Court of Auditors), a deputy and a senator, a local elected official, a university professor, the Chairman of the National Data Protection Commission and 4 qualified persons in various fields of expertise.

In practice, the UK Information Commissioner has a previous career as consumer rights lawyer, while his two assistants have worked for trade unions and local government. A Hungarian Information Commissioner has professional experience as lawyer and a professor of political science, and he has worked to promote the right to information. The Irish and Slovenian Information Commissioners were journalists who had worked on political and media freedom issues. Mexico has included among its Information Commissioners academics, lawyers, and individuals who have been working in public administration.

The composition of OECD oversight bodies for access to information tends to be representative of the citizenry of the country. In the case of the Belgian CARDA, for example, apart from its president, it has as many French-speaking as Flemish-speaking members with voting rights. In addition, the presidency is held alternately by a French-speaking and a Flemish-speaking person.

The clear majority of the CATI's members come from government and administration, which is consistent with its administrative and consultative nature. This composition differs from that of OECD access to information oversight bodies which, even when they have purely advisory functions and are competent only for administration, have a more representative composition of society and often include professors and judges.

In summary, it is recommended:

- To determine in the legislation precisely the number and categories of persons who may be members of the CATI;

- To ensure better balanced composition of the CATI by appointing members of parliament from the majority and the opposition and more members of civil society, the academic sector and judges;

- To establish a public and open procedure for the nomination, examination and appointment of members of the CATI;

- To limit the number of members of the commission to fifteen to preserve its effectiveness.

Collegiality and autonomy

CATI collegiality and autonomy

Collegial entity

Resolution of the Government of the Republic of Kazakhstan of 31 December 2015 No. 1175 provides that: […] "3. The activity of the Commission shall be carried out on the basis of openness and transparency in discussing and solving issues within its competence." […] "7. The Commission is chaired by the chairperson or his/her deputy. A meeting of the Commission shall be considered valid in the presence of at least two thirds of its members." […] "8. The members of the Commission shall be entitled to: 1) submit proposals for the agenda of the Commission meeting; 2) speak at the meeting and initiate voting on the proposals submitted; 3) familiarise themselves with the materials of the Commission work and obtain copies thereof." […] 14. Decisions of the Commission shall be taken through open voting and considered adopted if the majority of the total membership of the Commission have voted for it."

These provisions create a collegial institution. In this format, decisions are put to a vote. However, the voting rules (such as matters put to a vote, voting deadlines, special majorities, etc.) are not precisely determined by the resolution. In addition, since the majority members of the CATI are ministers or public officials, the government's view could in principle always prevail.

It should be noted that in the case of operating regulations of several OECD countries, for instance France and Italy, these rules are precisely determined to ensure that decisions are taken in a collegial, truly informed and well-considered manner.

Autonomy

Resolution of the Government of the Republic of Kazakhstan of 31 December 2015 n° 1175 provides that: "[…] 9. The Ministry shall be the working body of the Commission. The working body of the Commission in accordance with the procedure established by law shall: 1) provide organisational and technical support to the work of the Commission; 2) prepare proposals on the agenda of the Commission meeting, necessary documents and materials; 3) request necessary information from owners of information relevant to the activity of the Commission; 4) submit proposals for the improvement of the Commission activity to the Government of the Republic of Kazakhstan; 5) involve employees of other government authorities in its work, where necessary."

Administrative autonomy

It follows from these provisions of Article 9 that the CATI is not part of the Ministry of Information and Communications' structure. The Ministry is only the working body of the Commission and responsible for providing organisational and technical support to the Commission's work, the preparation of proposals, necessary documents, and materials on the agenda of the Commission's meeting. In addition, the CATI has no legal and autonomous personality, as it sits administratively under the Ministry of Information and Communications. These provisions cause some legal uncertainty.

Hierarchical submission to the Ministry of Information and Communications is problematic, since the CATI is chaired by the Deputy Prime Minister, who is the hierarchical superior of the Minister of Information.

The liability regime for CATI acts is unclear. During its activity, this body could commit acts that are harmful to third parties. Such persons may then wish to seek compensation for such damage. The CATI has no legal personality of its own and as such, it cannot be prosecuted before a court. At the same time, according to information received from the Kazakh authorities, the CATI's acts do not entail the responsibility of the administration, which cannot therefore be prosecuted for these acts. As a result, a victim of damage resulting from the CATI's actions would not be able to obtain compensation for that damage. In contrast to this situation, in OECD countries the prevailing principle is that a victim of damage should always be able to claim compensation for the damage, if necessary with the assistance of a judge.

For these reasons, it is recommended:

- To clarify the hierarchical line of the CATI;

- To determine the liability regime for its acts.

Decision-making autonomy

Decisions of the CATI are taken by a majority of its members. It is therefore necessary to assess the autonomy of each CATI member when voting.

For example, ministers are bound by government solidarity and discipline. Public officials represent the interests of the State and the body that nominated them, and are thus bound by their hierarchical subordination. Deputies of the Mazhilis of the Parliament of the

Republic of Kazakhstan have parliamentary immunity and are independent in making decisions within the framework of the current legislation of the Republic of Kazakhstan. It can be assumed that civil society representatives vote autonomously.

As majority of the CATI members belong to government and administration or the public sector, it is likely that the CATI is not autonomous from government and administration.

The obligations of the CATI members

Neither the law nor the resolution establish special rules for CATI members to avoid conflicts of interest or other forms of undue influence, nor do they demand that any declaration of assets and interests be submitted by CATI members.

It is therefore the ordinary law that applies to CATI members in this matter. At present, the declaration of income and property at the place of residence to the tax authority is a duty of civil servants in accordance with the Law of the Republic of Kazakhstan on Combating Corruption. However, not all Commission members are civil servants, but represent other organisations. It should be noted that a universal declaration of income and property is slated for introduction in the Republic of Kazakhstan on January 1, 2020.

Collegiality and autonomy of oversight bodies of OECD countries

Administrative and decision-making autonomy

Access to information oversight bodies in OECD countries enjoy wide operational and decision-making autonomy. Some bodies are established as a constitutional provision, such as the Swedish (Chapter 12 of the Regeringsform) and Danish (§55 of the Constitution) ombudsman. The National Institute for Transparency, Access to Information and Protection of Personal Data in Mexico is also a constitutional body. Because of this origin, those bodies are not under direct influence of the executive, legislative and judicial powers.

Most OECD countries' access to information oversight bodies are "quasi autonomous non-governmental organisations". They are created by the constitution or the law, and directed by an individual or a deliberative council. They have separate legal personality and are not subject to the ministerial hierarchy. They act through proposals, opinions, regulations, individual decisions and sanctions. This describes the operations of French, Italian and Belgian federal access to information administrative commissions, Canadian and German information commissioners. The OGIS of the United States of America, for its part, was established within the National Archives and Registries of the United States Administration, which has been an independent agency of the United States since 1985.

Functional connections

Concerning their activity, some OECD countries' access to information oversight bodies are functionally linked to a minister or an administrative department. This connection does not deprive them of their autonomy of decision and action.

Institutions reporting to the executive branch

Some access to information oversight bodies in OECD countries are attached to the President of the Republic, the Prime Minister, various ministries or administrative services, such as the national archives. This is often a functional link, i.e. for its management, the oversight body is integrated into the administrative services of a ministry, for example, the ministry of justice. However, it does not mean that it is dependent on the minister and his/her political decision-making process. For instance, the Japan Disclosure and Privacy Review Commission is an independent agency attached to the Ministry of the Interior and Communications. Similarly, the Office of the Australian Information Commissioner (OAIC) is an independent agency within the Australian Attorney General's Office.

Institutions reporting to the parliament

In accordance with the constitutional principle of the separation of powers, parliament exercises oversight over the executive power. In its task of monitoring the executive branch and the administration, some access to information oversight bodies in OECD countries assist parliament. As such, some access to information oversight bodies are attached to Parliament, such as the Commission for Access to Administrative Documents of Portugal, which sits in the Assembly of the Republic.

The obligations of members of bodies of OECD countries

Access to information oversight bodies in the OECD countries are subject to strict obligations to guarantee the proper performance of their professional duties. Provided for by the legislation, these conditions include civil and political rights, at the time of appointment, during, and even after the end of their mandates.

Members must show dignity and honour, both in their professional and personal lives. They are also subject to strict limitations. For instance, except for elected political members, they cannot exercise political mandates and, in several countries, their mandates are not renewable. They often are bound by the strictest respect for discretion and secrecy about information they may have acquired during their duties. In this way, members of the Japanese Information Disclosure and Privacy Review Commission are liable for sanctions if they disclose any information acquired during or after their term. These persons are often subject to oversight of their assets and any conflicts of interest that may affect the regular performance of their duties. They are prohibited from receiving instructions during the processing of cases and requests for opinions or appeals.

Mechanisms guaranteeing the transparency of the oversight bodies are also being put in place, for example by giving the widest publicity of their meetings and hearings. The aim for impartiality is reflected in rules that allow a member of that body to abstain at his/her own request, or even to be disqualified at the request of a party to the proceedings.

In conclusion:

- Unlike access to information collegial institutions in OECD countries, the commission operates in a highly regulated manner;

- The CATI's decision-making capacity and functional autonomy is weak in Kazakhstan, whereas it is very strong for institutions in OECD countries;

- The definition of the professional obligations of CATI members is very vague, whereas the definition of those of members of institutions in OECD countries are numerous and strict;

- A change in the CATI's status should lead to a revision of these clauses.

References

Commission for Access to Administrative Documents in France (2011), *Commission d'accès aux documents administratifs, Rapport d'activité* https://www.ladocumentationfrancaise.fr

Chapter 3. Mandate of the oversight body for access to information

General objectives of the Commission

Resolution of the Government of the Republic of Kazakhstan of 31 December 2015 No. 1175 provides that: "5. The main objectives of the Commission shall include: 1) develop proposals on the issues of access to information; 2) consider proposals and review the practice of implementing the legislation of the Republic of Kazakhstan in social relations linked to access to information that does not relate to sensitive information; 3) develop recommendations based on the analysis of the practice of implementing the legislation of the Republic of Kazakhstan in social relations linked to access to information that does not relate to sensitive information."

It should be noted that the terms of this article are quite abstract and need to be clarified to facilitate their application.

The CATI's jurisdiction is limited to access to information

As noted above, in certain OECD countries, legislation on access to information and on the protection of personal data is distinct, and different bodies oversee their implementation (e.g. France, Portugal, Italy). On the other hand, in several OECD countries, only one law or two laws apply to the right of access to information and the protection of personal data, but only one body is responsible for both legislations (e.g. UK, Germany, and Canada).

In Kazakhstan, the Parliament has passed two different laws: the Personal Data Protection Act and the ATIL. In accordance with the Law on Internal Affairs of the Republic of Kazakhstan, the institutions responsible for internal affairs ensure the protection of personal data. The CATI is therefore only competent for access to information, and it is incompetent for data protection. However, these provisions should not prevent the CATI from establishing relationships with institutions responsible for the enforcement of the Data Protection Act. More generally, the Kazakhstan government should consider establishing an institution to ensure the protection of personal data.

Relationship between access to information and data protection

The relationship between the right of access to information and the protection of personal data is very close, which explains why in most OECD countries, the same body is responsible for both. Even in the countries of this organisation where two different bodies deal with these domains, close cooperation exists and sometimes representatives of one body sit on the other. For instance, Italian law foresees that in the event of refusal of a request for access to documents for grounds of personal data protection, the Commission for Access to Administrative Documents must, before deciding on the applicant's appeal, request the opinions and considerations of the Guarantor Authority for the Protection of Personal Data. The French Law of 7 October 2016 organised the cooperation between the data protection body, the *Commission nationale de l'informatique et des libertés* (CNIL) and the CADA. The presidents of both institutions now sit on both boards. Moreover, the

CNIL and the CADA may, at the joint initiative of their chairs and when a subject of common interest justifies it, meet in a joint session as a single body.

As explained above, for the infringements of the law on personal data protection occurring in Kazakhstan, the prosecutor's office is responsible for enforcing that law.

In summary, it is recommended that:

- While respecting independence from the judiciary, establishing a regular exchange of information between the CATI and the Ministry of Justice on the application of the ATIL;

- Creating close relations between the CATI and the institutions responsible for internal affairs to ensure the protection of personal data, and organising joint actions, such as the sharing of information and experiences.

Considering the creation of an entity in charge of personal data protection

As stated above, Kazakh law on Personal Data Protection did not establish a designated body to monitor the law's implementation. In contrast, all OECD countries have set up such institutions. The tasks of these bodies are summarised as follows:

- Informing people about their rights and obligations and helping them exercise their rights;

- Regulating and identifying files and authorising the processing of the most sensitive data before their implementation;

- Ensuring that citizens are informed of, and have easy access to the data contained in processing operations concerning them;

- Monitoring compliance with the law;

- Sanctioning violations of the law;

- Understanding and anticipating developments in information technologies and being able to assess the consequences for the exercise of citizens' rights and freedoms

International experiences, and those of OECD countries, show that such personal data protection institutions are indispensable because of the importance of data in people's lives and the risks that an improper data usage may entail for them and for the rule of law.

It is therefore recommended to establish an independent data protection institution in Kazakhstan.

CATI's activities

Activity and practical operations

Since the CATI's inception in December 2015, meetings have taken place at least once every year. The meetings' agendas have included discussions of the proposals of non-governmental organisations to amend and supplement legislation on access to information, including the Regulation on the Commission's Procedures, the strategy for the development of the "Open Government" web portals, the results of public monitoring of compliance with the Law on Access to Information, conducted by the Ministry of Information and Communications of the Republic of Kazakhstan.

Based on the results of the meetings, decisions were taken, aiming, among other things, at popularising the "Open Government" web portals among the population, providing information holders with access to information, providing online broadcasting of open meetings of the Houses of Parliament and elected councils on official Internet resources, and facilitating the adaptation of official Internet resources for users with disabilities.

In 2019, the CATI has planned to review the results of the on-going law enforcement analysis of the Law on Access to Information, considering *inter alia* the recommendations of the present report, the results of the audit of the information systems of state bodies, and the creation of a single platform for Internet resources of state bodies.

Operating rules of the CATI

As purely consultative body that does not hear appeals against the refusal of access to information, CATI's operating rules are consistent with those of OECD countries.

Resolution of the Government of the Republic of Kazakhstan of 31 December 2015 No.1175 concerning the approval of the Regulation on the Rules of Procedure of the Commission for Access to Information is precise and clear:

- Article 6: "[…] The Commission chairperson shall lead the work of the Commission, approve the agenda of a regular meeting of the Commission, convene its meetings, where necessary, sign the minutes of the Commission meetings."

- Article 9: "The Ministry shall be the working body of the Commission. The working body of the Commission in accordance with the procedure established by law shall: 1) provide organisational and technical support to the work of the Commission; 2) prepare proposals on the agenda of the Commission meeting, necessary documents and materials; 3) request necessary information from owners of information relevant to the activity of the Commission; 4) submit proposals for the improvement of the Commission activity to the Government of the Republic of Kazakhstan; 5) involve employees of other government authorities in its work, where necessary."

- Article 11: "Meetings of the Commission shall be held as necessary but no more than once a half-year."

- Article 12: "Based on the results of the Commission meetings the secretary of the Commission shall draw up the minutes to be signed by the chairperson or deputy chairperson of the Commission and the secretary of the Commission."

- Article 15: "Recording and storage of materials and protocol decisions of the Commission shall be maintained by the working body of the Commission".

- Article 14: "Decisions of the Commission shall be taken through open voting and considered adopted if the majority of the total membership of the Commission have voted for it."

Procedure for preparing the meetings

The CATI's agenda for an upcoming meeting is formed by its working body, i.e. the Ministry of Information and Communications, and approved by its Chairman. The agenda is based on issues arising during the Ministry's activities in the field of access to information and law enforcement practices, as well as proposals from the CATI's members or requests from individuals and legal entities to provide access to information made to the Ministry as the working body of the Commission.

Procedure for opinions

According to the Regulations on the procedure, the CATI's members may independently submit proposals for the meeting's agenda to the Ministry (without having to request the working body of the Commission, i.e., the Ministry). The draft agenda of the meeting is sent by the secretary to members three days before the CATI's meeting.

At the same time, according to the amendments made to the Regulation on the Commission's procedure, if there will be decisions on the issues to be discussed at the meeting that are not provided for in the draft agenda, the secretary of the Commission shall draw up a new draft agenda that will be sent to the members of the Commission for voting. Thus, the opinions and decisions of the Commission's members are fixed in the minutes of meeting.

Official procedure for the implementation of the CATI's recommendations

The Commission's decisions are of a recommendatory nature. Protocol decisions taken at the meeting of the Commission are sent for execution to state bodies and organisations. It must be noted that most of the decisions taken to date by the Commission concerned the Ministry itself.

In addition, according to the amendments being made to the Regulation on the Commission's procedure, its Chairman exercises overall control over the implementation of its decisions.

OECD practice

In OECD countries and based on the principles of due process, it is possible to say that the proceedings before the oversight bodies guarantee:

- the right to be heard by a competent, independent and impartial oversight body;
- the right to a public hearing;
- the right to be heard within a reasonable time;
- the right to counsel;
- the right to interpretation.

In these countries, depending on tradition and legislation, the oversight bodies establish formal procedures for the introduction, examination and decision on access to information, both for general matters and for those concerning one or more persons. To ensure the quality and impartiality of their individual decisions, the decision-making procedure adopted by oversight bodies, particularly collegial bodies or commissions, often resembles that of a court. Decision-making is guided by the following principles:

- Oversight bodies' operating rules are based on their own legislation and other relevant legislation.
- Internal operating rules (oversight body internal rules, code of ethics, rules of procedure of the judging body) are adopted.

- The meetings of the decision-making organisation of the oversight institution for access to information are held according to the agenda communicated in advance by the responsible authority; a secretariat prepares the documents for the meetings; the chairman directs the work; voting regulations are applied; a register of deliberations is drawn up; an individual from the oversight institution is appointed to implement the decision.

- As regards individual cases, the procedure before the institution for access to information depends on the legal traditions of the OECD countries. The procedure may be written or oral. It is also very often conducted in the presence of both parties. This latter principle means that each party has the right to be informed of the other party's arguments and submissions. It also implies that the decision of the supervisory bodies will only be based on findings of which the parties to the proceedings are aware. Finally, the procedure may be inquisitorial or adversarial. In the inquisitorial procedure (for instance, in France), the access to information oversight body conducts the investigation. In adversarial proceedings (for example, in Canada), the claimant and the respondent entity are equal, the oversight body being limited to arbitrating the dispute between the two parties.

In summary, it would therefore be advisable for the CATI to adopt the principles of due process. The CATI must enact clear and stable rules of procedure and an adversarial decision-making procedure, with the presence of a rapporteur who prepares the case under review, presents it, and does not take part in the vote on the case.

Similarly, it is recommended that the schedule and programme of meetings be made public, allowing all stakeholders to participate in the procedure. The CATI's opinions should include all the legal and factual elements necessary for dealing with the subject. Moreover, the decision must be made public and accessible to all citizens. Finally, opinions received on the decisions must be made public as well.

Chapter 4. Review mechanisms

Means for reviewing refusals to provide information

Article 18 of ATIL provides: "1. Decisions and actions (inactions) of information holders, including a governmental body, a local self-government, an organisation, an official, a public servant, violating the rights of information users may be appealed against in a superior body, to a superior official, in the Republic of Kazakhstan, and/or in court."

According to the current Law on Access to Information and the Regulations on the Procedure for the Activity of the Commission, the CATI does not have the authority to review complaints and appeals by legal entities and individuals of an information holder's refusal to provide information. That competence is assigned to the government itself and to the judiciary.

Administrative and judiciary means of reviewing a refusal to provide information

Pursuant to the aforementioned Article 18 of the ATIL, there are two categories of appeal:

- Administrative, including a hierarchical appeal to superior body or a superior official;

- Judiciary, by filing an appeal.

The information's user may also choose how to complain of a violation of the right to access to information. These means of appeal can be used in parallel.

The Kazakhstan Human Rights Commissioner's intervention

The Human Rights Commissioner is the Kazakhstan Ombudsman. It monitors the observance of the human rights and freedoms and takes measures to restore violated rights and freedoms. It is appointed by the President of the Republic of Kazakhstan and is independent in carrying out its activities. The ATIL does not provide a role for the Human Rights Commissioner in monitoring or overseeing implementation.

In several OECD countries, the Ombudsman oversees implementing the law on access to information (e.g., in Sweden, Finland, Norway, Denmark, and New Zealand). This independent authority is responsible for examining citizens' complaints against the administration. As it is not part of the administration that denied access to information and against which the individual is complaining, the use of an ombudsman is beneficial. This system is satisfactory for the countries that use it.

In OECD countries, it is also customary for all institutions involved in access to information to meet and exchange information and experiences. For example, Canada's Information and Privacy Commissioners and Ombudspersons created a resolution to describe the models for collaboration among their institutions.

It is recommended that:

- In the context of its competencies, the Human Rights Commissioner takes a general interest in issues relating to access to information;

- The CATI should also establish on-going relationships with the Human Rights Commissioner to promote access to information and develop synergies.

Administrative liability

According to Article 18 of the ATIL, an unlawful restriction of the right to access to information may be appealed to a higher state body or to a court. In Kazakh law, complaints against the actions or inaction of officials, as well as decisions of state bodies, are submitted to a higher-ranking official or body or to the court no later than three months after the citizen became aware of the commission of an action or decision by the relevant official or body. If the appeal period expires, this does not constitute grounds for a state body or official or court to refuse to hear a complaint. The reasons for missing the deadline are clarified when the complaint is examined on the merits and can be one of the grounds for refusing to satisfy the complaint.

In accordance with Article 456-1 of the Code of the Republic of Kazakhstan on Administrative Offenses, administrative liability is foreseen for an illegal restriction of the right to access to information.

The unlawful refusal to provide information or the provision of knowingly false information in cases where such information is subject to provision at the request of the user of information in accordance with the legislation of the Republic of Kazakhstan, with the exception of actions for which liability is provided for by other articles of this code, shall be sanctioned by fines.

Knowingly publishing false information in the mass media, on the Internet resource of the information owner, on the Internet portal of open data or in other ways provided by the legislation, likewise entails fines that are categorized into groups.

The illegal attribution of limited access to information, except for actions provided for by part three of Article 504 of this code, entails a penalty for officials in the amount of twenty units;

The acts provided for by parts 1 and 2 of this article, committed repeatedly within a year after the imposition of an administrative penalty, entail a fine.

Without a thorough evaluation, the system of judicial review of violations of the right of access to information may appear satisfactory, because it is exercised by an institution independent of the administration, in accordance with the judicial procedure that is designed to guarantee the rights of individuals.

However, it is worth recalling the reasons that led the OECD countries to introduce an alternative method in this domain to recourse to the courts: the simplicity, speed, and economy of the review by an institution dedicated specifically to this function, which must also be independent of the administration which has refused access to information.

References

Website of the Permanent Mission of the Republic of Kazakhstan to the United Nations. Website accessed on September 13, 2018 http://kazakhstanun.com/kazakhstan-policy/kazakhstan-human-rights/

Website of the Office of the Information Commissioner of Canada. Website accessed on September 13, 2018 http://www.oic-ci.gc.ca/eng/2013-reading-room-other-documents-of-interests-2013-salle-de-lecture-autres-documents-interests_4.aspx

Chapter 5. Developing the Commission on Access to Information

Measures to improve the CATI's operation and the application of the ATIL that do not require legislative changes

Framing the CATI's strengthened mandate

OECD recommendations for a national open government strategy to ensure better good governance outcomes in Kazakhstan frame the recommendations for the CATI's strengthening. These recommendations include

- "Developing a full-fledged open government strategy [on Open government] (a single document) that includes principles, long-term goals, medium-term objectives, strategy instruments or initiatives to be carried out to achieve the goals. The strategy could also include the challenges, risks and threats that the country may face when implementing an open government strategy."

- "Ensuring that the open government agenda is both officially and practically one of the key priorities of the newly established Ministry for Information and Communications and that there are necessary mechanisms, human and financial resources to support this task and ensure the co-ordination of the new Ministry of Information and Communications with the presidency and the Central of Government."

- "Strengthening the necessary institutions, mechanisms and provide the necessary human and financial resources to ensure that the qualities and functions of the Central of Government are properly operationalised in order to ensure that open government strategy is successful and sustainable in the long term". (OECD, 2017a)

It is possible to make these principles operational by drawing up an action plan or roadmap which addresses the following sections:

- Describing the background and the rationale for the action plan.

- Defining goals, to clarify what is to be achieved by implementing these actions.

- Listing and prioritising the foreseen activities to achieve the goals and objectives.

- Defining which institution is in charge of the project and accountable for its implementation. Other actors who may be involved in implementing activities should also be specified.

- What resources are available such, as the financial resources (the budget to finance implementation of activities) and human resources.

- Setting start and end dates and specific milestones with deliverables.

- Setting the criteria for success. These will validate the success of an activity, or highlight the necessary corrections and lead to a new decision, and to the evolution of the action plan.

The content of this action plan could gain from the lessons learned in OECD countries. For instance, the strategic plan of the United Kingdom Information Commissioner aims to increase the trust the public has in government, public bodies and the private sector, and trust in transparency, in the digital economy and in digital public service delivery (United Kingdom Information Commissioner web site: https://ico.org.uk/) .

Its strategic approach highlights a commitment to:

- Lead the implementation and effective oversight of the GDPR and other live data protection reforms;

- Explore innovative and technologically agile ways of protecting privacy;

- Strengthen transparency and accountability and promote good information governance;

- Protect the public in a digital world

The 2018-19 Corporate Plan of the Office of the Australian Information Commissioner contains detailed programming of the actions it will undertake to fulfil its mandate Box 5.1).

Box 5.1. Office of the Australian Information Commissioner

Corporate Plan 2018-19: Key deliverables for 2018-19

"These priority projects, initiatives and actions will help us to achieve our Purpose in the coming year. To help us promote and uphold privacy rights we will:

- Continue to administer the Notifiable Data Breaches scheme, and work with key stakeholders to build business and government capacity to reduce the potential for and to respond to data breaches, and to assist individuals who are affected by a data breach.

- Engage in the development and prepare for commencement of the Consumer Data Right and work collaboratively with the Australian Competition and Consumer Commission.

- Work collaboratively with the National Data Commissioner to assist in the development of a new data sharing and release framework.

- Work with credit providers, credit reporting bodies, consumers and external dispute resolution schemes to help ensure that changes to credit reporting under the proposed mandatory Comprehensive Credit Reporting regime are implemented in a way that protects the privacy of individuals and facilitates an efficient credit reporting system.

- Update existing guidance where required and develop new guidance on privacy rights and obligations.

- Use our discretionary regulatory powers in a proportionate and targeted way to ensure the protection of personal data.

- Support compliance with the Australian Government Agencies Privacy Code.

- Conduct targeted assessments in priority areas to monitor and improve privacy practices.

- Promote Privacy Awareness Week 2019.To help us promote and uphold information access rights we will:

- Continue the development of our early resolution process to improve the review time of Information Commissioner reviews and to further meet the objectives of providing an informal, non-adversarial and timely review process.

- Update resources for applicants to help them understand the Information Commissioner review process.

- Update resources for agencies and ministers to support best practice decision making.

- Support FOI officers through the provision of communication materials, training and advice.

- Continue to participate in the Open Government Forum, and contribute to the development and implementation of Australia's next Open Government National Action Plan.

- Review the administration of the Information Publication Scheme and disclosure logs by agencies and ministers.

- Monitor agencies' compliance with the statutory decision-making timeframes, as set out in the FOI Act.

- Conduct a campaign for Right to Know Day

Source: Office of the Australian Information Commissioner Corporate Plan 2018–19, https://www.oaic.gov.au/resources/about-us/corporate-information/key-documents/corporate-plan-2018-19.pdf

The principles provided by the World Bank, presented in Box 5.2, could also serve as an example.

Box 5.2. 5 Principles of the World Bank's New Access to Information Policy

1. Maximizing Access: Disclose any information in the Bank's possession that is not covered by a list of exceptions. Most restricted information to be declassified over time.

2. Clear Exceptions: Deny access to information whose disclosure may harm "well-defined interests" that are identified in a set of exceptions.

3. Safeguarding Deliberative Process: While being "fully open" about decisions, results, and agreements, deliberations that lead to these outcomes are considered confidential.

4. Clear Disclosure Procedures: Routinely post as much information "as practical" to the Bank's external website. Clearly defined procedures for requesting information and processing requests, including timelines.

5. Right to Appeal: Provide a two-stage appeals process for denied requests –an internal mechanism and a second, external body.

Source: World Bank http://www.bankinformationcenter.org/wp-content/uploads/2013/01/InfoBrief_Mar2010.pdf

Ensuring the functioning of the Commission

The ministry of information and communications' capacity and functions concerning ATIL oversight and implementation

Meetings of the Commission are held as necessary. According to amendments adopted in June 2018, the regularity shall be no less than once in every quarter of the year. Thus, it is necessary to guarantee that the Ministry of Information and Communications can fulfil its responsibilities to the CATI. An evaluation should therefore be conducted on the staff available and of the administrative organisation dedicated fulfilling the functions entrusted to them

Establishing an annual CATI work programme and making it widely known

This document must present a political vision of the commission's work, the actions it will lead, and the means it will use. It must also establish a work schedule, setting priorities and identifying the persons responsible for their implementation.

This document must be constantly updated and disseminated through the various means of communication available, for example, through the press or their websites, as done, for example, by the United Kingdom Information Commission.

Clarifying the CATI's legal responsibility

In its activities, the CATI may commit acts harmful to third parties, for instance, due to incorrect information contained in its resolutions. The current liability regime for these acts is not clear. To ensure the CATI's functioning in accordance with the rule of law it is recommended that the Kazakh authorities determine the conditions of engagement of the CATI's liability and the court competent to rule on any disputes in this matter.

Improving the CATI's internal operating rules

The CATI is an administrative commission with an advisory purpose, but which is not authorised to rule on individual decisions regarding the refusal of access to information. It is therefore fundamentally different from the oversight bodies in OECD countries. However, while respecting the Resolution, to give more credibility to its action, its mode of operation could be brought closer to that of oversight bodies in OECD countries.

Hence, the CATI could:

- adopt the principles of due process;

- enact clear and stable rules of procedure, using an adversarial decision-making procedure, with a rapporteur who prepares the case under consideration, presents it and does not take part in the vote on the case;

- publicise the schedule and programme of meetings in advance;

- allow all stakeholders to intervene in the procedure;

- produce opinions that include all the legal and factual elements necessary for dealing with the subject;

- make the CATI's opinions and opinions received on the decisions public and accessible to all citizens.

Creating a system to monitor the CATI's decisions

The CATI should establish an inventory of these decisions. The holders of the information to whom these decisions are addressed should inform the CATI of the measures they have taken to carry out these acts. Depending on the responses it receives, the CATI may decide to reconsider the case and reformulate a new decision.

Drafting an annual activity report

Access to information institutions in the OECD countries are accountable to citizens and governments for their activities. They fulfil this obligation by various means, including annual activity reports. For instance, the German Federal Commissioner for Data Protection and Freedom of Information gives in his report an overview of the priority activities for the two-year period and a perspective on the key data protection issues that lie ahead.

It is recommended that CATI prepare an annual activity report. This document would provide statistics and analyses on the implementation of access to information legislation, review legislative and regulatory developments, report on the CATI's activity and evaluate its performance, and address thematic issues of importance to the institution.

Making the legislation uniform across the public administration and facilitating its application by public institutions

OECD countries place the utmost importance on the uniform application of the law by the various institutions involved in the right of access to information. Access to information legislation is relatively new in Kazakhstan. It requires even more effort to disseminate and clarify its application, by coordinating and aligning the functions of different public institutions that are obliged to enforce the law.

In summary, the recommended actions are:

- Making CATI opinions and recommendations publicly available, especially via the Internet. Nevertheless, the CATI should respect privacy principles, for example, by making published decisions anonymous.

- Creating a database and statistics on the application of the Access to Information Act. The data base and statistics could include information items as described below:

  - For general cases managed by CATI, it is necessary to record the type of file (whether it is examination of a draft text, or a decree, or law); the nature of the referral to the CATI; author of the referral to CATI; the activity concerned by the referral; the region or city; the date of the CATI's receipt of the referral; the date of the CATI's resolution; and the nature of the CATI's resolution.

- For access to information requests, it is necessary to record: the author of the request; the administration concerned by the request; the activity concerned by the request; the response to the request (favourable, partially favourable, or the refusal of the request); appeal procedures against a decision of total or partial refusal of access to information (hierarchical appeal, ombudsman, or judicial); the decision of the appeal authority; the judicial appeal against the decision of the appealed authority; the judicial decision; and all dates.

- Monitoring the case law of other bodies working in the field of access to information.

- Establishing a method for classifying the case law of all actors involved in the field of access to information.

- Drafting and publishing thematic fact sheets. These documents present important issues about access to information and emphasise key points concisely, using tables, bullet points and/or headings, on a single printed page. They must be updated periodically, to enable administrations to respond to requests for access to information.

- Posting an access to information request form template on the CATI website, and for each public institution subject to the ATIL.

- Preparing and updating government directives and instructions to the administration on the implementation of access to information legislation and, within its jurisdiction, on the preservation of archives and documents. These documents must explain how the law and other regulations must be applied, by giving examples and analysing concretes situations. It is also necessary to keep documents in good condition, to prevent them from being damaged or destroyed. Finally, there is a need for a method of classifying archives and documents so that they can be consulted and used.

- Writing and publishing practical guides for information holders (public institutions) explaining how to respond to an access to information request.

- Creating a web simulation tool that assists administrations and informs access requesters about the legislation in the domains where the access to information doctrine is well established. For example, the French CADA website offers a simple simulation tool that helps administrations and informs applicants about the communicability of administrative documents.

Facilitating the relationship with individuals and entities responsible for access to information

The ATIL does not provide for the obligation to establish structural units or authorised officials for the purposes of organising access to public information.

However, most OECD countries have designated permanent structures or officials to organise access to information, which have proved to be very useful. The Kazakhstan government should therefore instruct its administration to designate these permanent structures or officials in administrative units where they have not yet been established.

The CATI could establish a network with the units or officials identified. For example, the CADA in France has created and coordinates a network of persons responsible for access to administrative documents in French administrations. The main tasks of these persons are to simplify the exercise of the right of access and re-use by users, to enable the administration to be better informed of the responses to be given to communication requests addressed to it, and to be CADA's points of contact for examining requests.

In Kazakhstan, these units or officials would become CATI correspondents for the access to information requests they receive. They could also seek its advice when they receive an access to information request. At the same time, they would be constantly informed by the CATI of the changes in law and practice, through regular information addressed to them. It is recommended to establish an Internet forum for making the network activities transparent, and to regularly organise training courses for network members.

Strengthening the CATI's links with its judicial and administrative partners

As explained in this report, several institutions are involved in the implementation of the right of access to information in Kazakhstan. It is therefore important to strengthen synergies between them to increase the efficiency of the system in the application of ATIL.

To this end, it is recommended to take the following actions:

- While respecting the independence of the judiciary, reinforcing exchange of information between the CATI and the Ministry of Justice on the application of the ATIL, for instance, by the regular transmission of statistics on the application of the ATIL, discussions on its difficulties of application and the necessary changes in legislation.

- Creating close relations between the CATI and the Ministry of Internal Affairs of Kazakhstan by organising joint actions, such as exchanges of information and experience.

- Inviting a representative of the Ministry of Internal Affairs of Kazakhstan to CATI meetings.

- Establishing on-going relationships with the Ombudsman for Human Rights in questions concerning access to information

Continuing to assess ATIL

It is necessary to continue, engaging with all the stakeholders, the evaluation of the text of the ATIL, its application and the challenges it raises. On the basis of this evaluation, it is recommended to draw up reform projects accompanied by impact assessments.

Reinforcing relations with civil society

In OECD countries, civil society organisations attach great importance to the right of access to information as an essential tool in their activities. It enables them, on the one hand, to understand the reasons for public action and to act on it, and, on the other, to act as a force for public proposals. At the same time, civil society and institutions responsible for access to information maintain a close dialogue. It is acknowledged that supporting each other creates value for both parties and contributes to common objectives, for example by disseminating legislation or by establishing joint training courses. Citizens are also mobilising and creating initiatives to monitor the implementation of the Access to Information and Data Protection Act in practice.

The CATI has already initiated exchanges with Kazakh NGOs working in the field of access to information. They should be continued and deepened, by organising exchange workshops, listening to their proposals and by making them aware of the government's projects in the field of access to information.

Bringing the CATI closer to Parliament

As important instruments for democracy, the bodies involved in exercising oversight of the right of access to information in OECD countries have close links with their parliaments. Some bodies are attached to parliament. All oversight bodies are subject to control by the legislature, either directly or through legislative oversight of the executive. In this way, the Portuguese CADA is subject to ordinary scrutiny by committees of the country's parliament. Similarly, when preparing the annual finance law, the latter examines its functioning. The Italian information oversight access body submits a report to Parliament. The Information Commissioner of Ireland is required to publish an annual report, tabled in each House of the National Parliament. The Hungarian and United Kingdom Information Commissioners report to Parliament on their work. The activity reports of the German Federal Commissioner for Data Protection and Freedom of Information are discussed in the Bundestag. In subsequent resolutions, the Bundestag expresses its opinion on major issues relating to the right to information and data protection.

The CATI could therefore present its annual report to the Kazakh Parliament, which could examine it and periodically question this institution on the application of legislation on the right of access to information and the necessary developments in case law.

Measures requiring legislative change

Considering the important differences between the oversight bodies for access to information in OECD countries and the CATI, some measures are recommended that require legislative changes.

Evolving the CATI's status

This recommendation concerns amendments to the CATI as an institution without fundamentally changing the access to information legislation.

Membership

- It is recommended to determine precisely the number of persons and categories they represent as members of the CATI;

- It is recommended to better balance the composition of the CATI by engaging more members representing civil society, the academic sector, and the judiciary.

- For the CATI to remain effective, its member count should not exceed fifteen.

Reinforcing the professional obligations of CATI members

The definition of the professional obligations and duties of CATI members are very general, while the definition of those of members of institutions in OECD countries are numerous and strict. Thus, it should be necessary to create for CATI's members:

- An ethics code on personal and professional conduct;

- A declaration of interest and assets.

Rebalancing voting rules

Currently, the clear majority of CATI members belong to the government. As a result, the CATI's decisions will likely follow the government's wishes. In OECD countries, the significant presence of independent figures in access to information oversight bodies (professors, judges, or representatives from NGOs) moderate government influence of their decisions.

It would therefore be appropriate for the Government of Kazakhstan to consider giving greater participation to independent professionals in the CATI.

Clarifying hierarchy in the Commission

Today, the CATI is under the Ministry of Information and Communications and chaired by the Deputy Prime Minister. As explained above, the role of the CATI as a distinctly independent institution is not legally clear. Thus, the hierarchical relation should be reorganised.

Recommendations to apply best practice according to international standards

The following recommendations suggest that Kazakhstan establish a genuine oversight body for access to information in accordance with all the criteria followed by the OECD countries.

An autonomous oversight bodies for access to information

As outlined in this report, Kazakhstan needs a truly autonomous oversight body. To bring Kazakh legislation into conformity with international principles of the right of access to information: (a) appeals against an information holder's decisions must be possible; (b) the appellate body should be independent and have the means to fulfil its task; it should have legal personality and operative, budgetary and decision-making autonomy; (c) this body could be a judicial or administrative structure; (d) if an administrative structure existed in addition to court procedures to ensure the rights, it would be preferable that this structure should be bound to report to the Parliament.

Currently, according to Kazakh legislation, the functions relating to freedom of information are listed as follows:

- General application of the access to Information Act is a role held by the CATI;

- Challenging refusals to respond positively to an access to information request can be carried out by way of hierarchical recourse and court proceedings;

- Monitoring of the law on the protection of personal data is the responsibility of institutions responsible for internal affairs, in accordance with the Law on Internal Affairs of the Republic of Kazakhstan.

- The complaint for an infringement of the Data Protection Act is addressed to the prosecutor's office when the infringement occurs in Kazakhstan; it is addressed to the Ministry of Internal Affairs of Kazakhstan or its territorial departments when the violation happens abroad.

It is recommended that Kazakh authorities should clarify the functions, including:

- Identifying precisely the information issues they wish to regulate. For example, one of the questions to be considered would be how to ensure, through a fair and independent procedure, the protection of the right of access to information of natural and legal persons.

- Determining whether existing bodies working in the right of access to information have the necessary legal, material and human resources to fulfil their roles.

- Considering whether the Commission's mandate should be modified by entrusting it with new functions related to access to information, such as deciding on appeals in the event of a refusal of access to information.

- Assessing the division of competencies regarding access to information between the institutions responsible for the protection of personal data and CATI, with a view to deciding whether it is appropriate to modify the powers of either of these institutions.

- Considering setting up an independent body to monitor legislation on the protection of personal data.

References

UK Information Commissioner website, accessed on 30 August 2018 https://ico.org.uk/media/about-the-ico/documents/2014134/20170413icoinformationrightsstrategicplan2017to2021v10.pdf

Canada Statistical Report on the Access to Information Act, https://www.tbs-sct.gc.ca/tbsf-fsct/350-62-html-eng.asp

Canadian Access to Information Manual, https://www.canada.ca/en/treasury-board-secretariat/services/access-information-privacy/access-information/access-information-manual.html)